Advance Praise for
Desire Returns for a Visit

"These are fresh poems in every sense of the word. Flirty, audacious, original. A fresh take on Dickinson's love of women and words. A brazen exploration of the life cycle of love affairs. This book is an open-mouthed kiss to the reader. It will leave you breathless."
~G.L. Morrison, poet, lover of words, and writer of short fiction

"[Sandra de Helen's] book of poems is a great way to read a truthful, witty, poignant memoir of lesbian love."
~Judy Grahn, poet, author, professor, and grande dame of lesbian poetry and nonfiction

"I didn't need to read beyond the first line of the first poem to know I'd be loving this book."
~Lee Lynch, novelist, essayist, short story writer, trailblazer, and both the inspiration and first winner of the annual Lee Lynch Classic Award given by the Golden Crown Literary Society

Desire Returns for a Visit
Intimate Poems about Lesbian Love

by

Sandra de Helen

2018

DESIRE RETURNS FOR A VISIT is a work of poetic fiction. Names, characters, places, and incidents are either the product of the author's imagination or are used fictitiously. Any resemblance to actual persons living or dead, business establishments, events, or locales is entirely coincidental. Further copyright notes can be found at the conclusion of the collection.

A Launch Point Press Trade Paperback Original

Copyright © 2018 by Sandra de Helen

All rights reserved. Launch Point Press supports copyright which enables creativity, free speech, and fairness. Thank you for buying the authorized version of this book and for following copyright laws by not using or reproducing any part of this book in any manner whatsoever, including Internet usage, without written permission from Launch Point Press, except in the form of brief quotations embodied in critical reviews and articles. Your cooperation and respect supports authors and allows Launch Point Press to continue to publish the books you want to read.

ISBN 978-1-63304-202-5

FIRST EDITION: First Printing, 2018

Editing: Luca Hart
Cover Design: Jove Belle

Portland, Oregon
www.LaunchPointPress.com

Dedication

This collection of poems about my experience of love as a lesbian is dedicated to every woman with whom I've had a love relationship that lasted more than a year. Affairs and one-night stands don't have much of an arc, do they? Mine didn't. There was attraction, a bit of fun, and then there wasn't. But relationships that lasted a year or more had a life. One relationship has lasted more than half the years I have lived. First we were friends for three years, then partners for nineteen years, and then friends again for the last fifteen years and counting. Here's to you, Pam.

To Joanie and to Bev: each of you will always have a special place in my heart; each of you helped me become the woman I am today.

Author's Foreword

This collection of poetry is arranged according to phases of a lesbian love relationship. I use *Becoming, Falling, Grappling, Breaking, Living,* and *Ending* as markers for the developmental stages of all relationships. You may think not all relationships end, but I assure you they do. If you're lucky, they end in death after a long, happy time together. The primary relationship I write about in this collection is one that lasted for nearly nineteen years as a committed, monogamous partnership. Before we became lovers, we were friends. After, we returned to being friends.

These poems were written over a period of seven years. Much of my own growth happened because I returned to poetry after a long sabbatical from the form. Distilling stories and feelings into metaphor, simile, and precise words allowed my emotions to expand, grow, and change.

Many of my poems are written as a response or reaction to poems by Emily Dickinson. (Each of those poems contain a poem by Emily Dickinson at the top; my own poem follows.) Some scholars believe Emily Dickinson fell in love with her sister-in-law, Susan. Many of her poems are written to Susan. Susan lived in the house next door to Emily Dickinson. They corresponded daily, sometimes more than once daily. When I read her poetry, I feel as if I'm reading work by a woman who loved women. My response poems (also known as *ekphratic* poems) are scattered throughout this collection.

I work to make my poetry accessible. I write to help readers reach their own stories, to touch their own feelings. Some refer to this genre of poetry as "confessional." I reject that label. I have nothing to confess. But I do have stories to disclose. We all do.

Sandra de Helen
November 2018

Contents

Becoming

Becoming Lesbian 1977 Version	1
Stealing with Permission	2
Beginnings	3

Falling

The First Time, After Emily Dickinson	7
Stars in My Eyes	8
Fifty Percent Have a List	9
Waiting for Inertia	10
How to Control Your Dreams	11
Don't Speak	12
you burn me	13
Taking a Personal Day	14
A Love Poem, After Emily Dickinson	15
A Lover's Rhyme: Steadfast Honey, After Emily Dickinson	16
Choice, After Emily Dickinson	17
No Map	19
Dry Season	20
Tarantism, n. an extreme impulse to dance	21
Is You IS or Is You Ain't	22
Honeymoon, After Emily Dickinson	23
How to Dance with a Bad Dancer	24
Mooning the Sun	25

Suspense, After Emily Dickinson	26
How to Influence Dreams	27
Spare	28
The Lovers, After Emily Dickinson	29
Tuxedo and Gown (Beautiful)	31
Desire Returns for a Visit	33
Possession, After Emily Dickinson	34
Night & Day, After Emily Dickinson	35
Celebration Time, After Emily Dickinson	36

Grappling

Ready to Dwell	39
Before Marriage Equality	40
In the Dark	42
Compensation, After Emily Dickinson	44
Valentine's Day Passion	45
How Do You Want To Be Saved?	46
The Air Up There, After Emily Dickinson	47
Dream of Heaven, After Emily Dickinson	48
Tweedledum and Tweedledee	49
Two Women Looking for Fifty States, or Marriage Equality	50
Texas	51
Thirty Years	52
Surrender	54
Birthday Celebration	56
Witnessing Marriage Equality	57

Breaking

Language of Flowers	61
Sweetbitter Unmanageable Creature	62
A Gift-Giving Occasion	63
Shimmering	64
That Faraway Look	65
Quitting Time, After Emily Dickinson	66
Too Soon Old, After Emily Dickinson	67
The Power of Love, After Emily Dickinson	68
Dependency, After Emily Dickinson	70
Loving a Survivor	72
Holding	73
Don't Forget	75
Crying in the Face of Rain	76
and then I said . . .	77
Donations	78
Looking through Stained Glass	79
Lost in Translation	80
Storms	81
You Hurt Me	82
Divorce	83
Use as Indicated	84
Pity Party	85
Keeping Apart, After Emily Dickinson	86
No Time Like the Present	87

Living

The Biology of Co-Dependent Love	91
Love Lifted Me	92
Apocalypse, After Emily Dickinson	93
Invitation	95
Last Dance of the Blue Moon	96
Do You Know the Way?	97
You Get What You Pay For (and pay for what you get)	98
You're Gone	99
Hope	100
Immortal Love, After Emily Dickinson	101
Both Sides Now, After Emily Dickinson	102
The Lost Jewel, After Emily Dickinson	103
The Contract, After Emily Dickinson	104
One is Enough, After Emily Dickinson	105

Epilogue

Dead Reckoning	109

Becoming

Becoming Lesbian 1977 Version

Wearing makeup is as unnecessary as painting crickets. Makeup is a tool of the patriarchy. If you paint your face wear dresses, wear your hair long, put on soft sweaters, silky blouses, you are doing it to attract men and you aren't a real lesbian. Anne will cut your hair. I'll take you to the thrift store for jeans and flannel shirts. You have to get rid of those skirts and heels, dresses, coats, hats, gloves, stockings, slips, nightgowns, and lingerie. You need cotton underwear and socks. Boots. You can have a pair of cotton Mary Janes from China for summer. (Thank Goddess! One femme item allowed!) I sure hope this transformation is worth it!

Stealing with Permission,
or coming out as a lesbian in the 1970s

You turn your lips to mine begging
me to steal a kiss, when all the time
I long for you to be the one to
steal a kiss from me.

Confusion reigns in this time of enforced
androgyny. Permission is granted for
free love, but there are rules which
wreak havoc with our ability to read
body language.

The signs say take me take me, but
how can we all take each other?

I write a permission slip and pin it to the
pocket of my flannel shirt. I wonder
who will read it when all these
women have their chins up and
their eyes shut?

Beginnings

The first step, the first day of
school, the first kiss, the first
job. The first time you fall in
love. The heat! The excitement!
The sleepless nights, the brand-
new feelings in parts of your
body, corners of your heart, the
razor burns, the blue suede fuzz
balls rubbed onto your new white
car coat. The first dance. The
song that is now your song, to
live forever in your memory as
the first time.

Long after that first step led you
to adventures, to missteps, to your
one true love—long after you left
school, retired from all the jobs of
your life, one bar of music from the
last song that was "your song," one
bar can summon up the heat, make
your old feet long to dance. You
can feel the strength of the arms of
your one true love again. You wrap
yourself in the sweater she left behind,

dance yourself into yet another new beginning.

Every day is the first day of the rest of your life.

Falling

6 | Desire Returns for a Visit

The First Time

> *Come slowly, Eden!*
> *Lips unused to thee,*
> *Bashful, sip thy jasmines,*
> *As the fainting bee,*
> *Reaching late his flower,*
> *Round her chamber hums,*
> *Counts his nectars—enters,*
> *And is lost in balms!*
> ~Emily Dickinson

I touched her hair—and was
lost, found, ensnared—she
pulled me to her and took my
lips.

I tasted her nectar. From the
first drop I was an addict, my
hunger was loosed, like a
crazed bee, I forgot my
dance to my hive.

I discovered Eden in her
embrace, then drowned in
her balms.

Stars in My Eyes

When I met you, I felt as innocent and ignorant as an infant. Everything I ever learned had to be erased and replaced with the truth of you and our love. All knowledge I thought I had I now had to unlearn. My world was new. Because of you.

You held me in such a way, I knew I was loved as a woman for the first time. My frozen heart shed its cage and reach for your own heart in order to beat in your rhythm. My skin, my hair, my limbs, my very soul became alive as if I were newly born.

When we looked at the sky together, no longer did I see constellations. I saw a velvet sky studded with diamonds. They mimicked the sparkle of your eyes when you saw me. That lighting of your face at my appearance lifted me. You were the stars in my firmament, the sun I spun around.

Fifty Percent Have a List

Put your list of love-making words on
the nightstand for later. You might want
to add to it afterward. I won't use your
words at first because my mouth will be
busy tasting you.

I won't speak except to say Mm or
maybe Ahh when I come up for air.
I won't be taking notes, because my
hands will be occupied touching, exploring,
and filling your body.

My feet will be finding purchase on the
bed, on the floor, or on the wall as I
find your lovely places.

Speak your special words. You have my
full attention. I want to hear you. I want
your words to stuff my ears, dribble down
my chin, spill across my chest, slip down
between my legs, and hide inside.

I want your words to penetrate, to go
deeper, harder, hotter. I want you.
I am listening.

Say anything.

Waiting for Inertia

Inertia doesn't come to those who wait. Good things do. There was no stopping her though, she wanted to change her name to Inertia and it was the 70s. I was merely a friend who longed to be her lover. I came out that spring and by summer I'd been with six women loving my way around town seeking someone compatible. I found it a bit difficult as we all looked alike. I couldn't discern the subtleties of the femme versus butch mannerisms yet, mainly because femmes were so busy being butch. Inertia resisted me harder than any other woman. I gave up after a weak fight. Now I laugh because she was so clearly a femme who could see me for what I was. She advised me to wait for the right woman.

How to Control Your Dreams

Sleep with one eye open.
Wrap your arms around your
pillow and hold on tight.
Spoon your lover, and lock
your arms around her waist.
Make a recording for yourself
directing your dream. Play it
on a loop.
Have someone sit beside you
throughout the night and tell
you what to dream.
Eat pizza for nightmares.
Eat candy for exciting thrillers.
Don't eat at all, but sleep with
crushed roses for erotic dreams.
Have no regrets, do nothing wrong,
be kind, be generous, relax and
all your dreams will be in
your control.

Don't Speak

Don't say a word, just close your
eyes, part your
lips, and let me hold your
head in my hand as my
lips touch yours and my
tongue brushes your
teeth seeking to silence
you for another
moment, give me another
brief interlude for the
story that lives in my
body when you are near me.
It begins as heat rising from
my center a breath quickening
my pulse racing my ears
straining to hear our
hearts beating in unison
my thighs reaching for
yours even when I'm still
seated still driving to
our destination the
hair on the back of your
neck calls the palm of my
hand like a magnet to a
pin. I'm helpless.
Let our warmth guide us.
No need for
words.

you burn me

you burn me with your flaming tresses
your lashes dragging across my alabaster cheek
you sear my groin with your tight curls
each a cinder against my skin
brave tortured warrior I remain
bound to you by the color of your hair.

azure eyes, rosy silken skin, lips
the shade of ripe peaches, those
I can pass by as a half-dry stream.
Breasts lightly straining against
your linen gown, an indented shape,
buttocks that draw my two hands.
no matter, I am strong, I will resist.

but your glossy locks, thick, shining
spilling like a waterfall of fire
I am lost as a lamb in the smoke
seeking its mother
branded as a calf going to
slaughter. My scars ache.

Taking a Personal Day

A lie in begins with a conversation.
You're awake when I open my eyes.
Three more days to go before the
weekend, I moan. You moan, but in
a different way. You open your
arms to me, and I roll in. Your breasts
are warm, soft pillows, up against my
stomach as my breasts are against your
chest. You open my thighs by nudging
them with your knee. Let's stay home
today, you push the words into my
ear with your tongue and hot breath.
I answer by sliding my hand down your
side to your hip, then dropping it down
to the back of that nudging knee. Oh
yes, we're having a lie in today.

A Love Poem

> *It's all I have to bring to-day*
> *This, and my heart beside,*
> *This, and my heart, and all the fields,*
> *And all the meadows wide.*
> *Be sure you count, should I forget,*
> *—Some one the sum could tell, —*
> *This, and my heart, and all the bees*
> *Which in the clover dwell.=*
> ~Emily Dickinson

Love is all I have to give you, and I give it all to you. My love, and my heart. My heart and the enormity of my soul.

The forests, the fields, the rivers and seas. The night skies filled with light from stars, suns, comets, planets to infinity. And more. The particles in the atmosphere that make our skies blue. The fish, the fowl, the flora and fauna. These make up the enormity of my soul, for I am but a vessel of atoms, joining all the other atoms of our universe.

This, and my heart, and my love. All I have to give. I give to you.

A Lover's Rhyme: Steadfast Honey

> *. . . Staring, bewildered, at the mocking sky.*
> *Homesick for steadfast honey,*
> *Ah! the bee flies not*
> *That brews that rare variety.*
> ~Emily Dickinson

My honey brings me toast and jam
and brews my special tea.
My honey sits tight by my side and
reads aloud to me.
My honey loves no other one
nor do I spread my wings.
We are each other's only love
we strum our own heartstrings.

Choice

So bashful when I spied her,
So pretty, so ashamed!
So hidden in her leaflets,
Lest anybody find;
So breathless till I passed her,
So helpless when I turned
And bore her, struggling, blushing,
Her simple haunts beyond!
For whom I robbed the dingle*,
For whom betrayed the dell,
Many will doubtless ask me,
But I shall never tell!
~Emily Dickinson

*A narrow dale or valley between hills.

The time for hiding our love, for
life in the shadows, that time is
over. We live among the people
for whom this world was built,
fashioned from their own moralistic
hands, excluding all whose love
is different from their own.

Now we can declare our love,
gather in twos or crowds to
witness our legal unions. Those
who fear us are now the ones
in the shadows, bearing arms

or barbed words to try to force
us back into the dark.

Let us sing of our love, and
keep our poetic voices. Let us
carry each other aloft, robbing
our dingles, betraying our dells,
telling everyone—including
ourselves.

No Map

You ask how I will find you without a map? I need no map
no GPS, not even a light to guide me. I am drawn by the scent of your breasts.

Dry Season

There's an *arroyo seco* right next to my
littoral zone. Crazy right? Dry bed adjacent
to an area so rich in love and light, plants
and animals, it could make a person
orgasmic. Can we slop some of that salty
moisture from the zone into our bed? The
dust is choking me. The rocks are sharp.
I long for the silky feel of oceanic blue
upon my parched skin. I dream in colors
of algae and starfish. Will you kindly
stagger away from the rain shadow and
let me dip your lips in the balm of warm
liquid? The sun reaches depths here you
may not have experienced. Its heat will
penetrate all the way to your sediment.
I've done everything but subduct you.
Kiss me, you fool.

Tarantism, n. an extreme impulse to dance

Our first Halloween. You dressed as a
sailor, and I was your slutty wench. I wore
heels, and a black dress with a slit up to
here. Here where you can feel my heart
beating for you, but later, later. The
Dyke Tones are singing, and I have an
uncontrollable urge to dance, to feel
your strong arms around me, to lay
my head on your shoulder, to press
my leg between yours in a slow dance
meant to lead to . . . later. Later, when
the dykes are no longer playing our
song, when the women are ready to
stagger out into the street in a throng.
Later when you take me home and oh
so slowly remove the dress, the torn
stockings, the fear from my heart that
you might not be the one.

Is You Is Or Is You Ain't

If you have to ask, the answer is probably ain't. I know cause my baby lets me know in every way you can't think of.

My baby does the housework, the dishes, the cooking, takes out the trash. and turns the fan on me when I need it. All without asking.

My baby gives me folding money, compliments my appearance, loves my smell. My baby sings our song on karaoke night and grins at me across the room of other women wishing for a baby like mine.

I don't have to ask. And neither does she.

Honeymoon

> *Wild nights! Wild nights!*
> *Were I with thee,*
> *Wild nights should be*
> *Our luxury! Futile the winds*
> *To a heart in port,—*
> *Done with the compass,*
> *Done with the chart.*
> *Rowing in Eden!*
> *Ah! the sea!*
> *Might I but moor*
> *To-night in thee!*
> ~Emily Dickinson

All those nights we lived
apart were calm, quiet, and
often lonely. I can but
dream of those wild nights
we were first together.

Sometimes I ride in the
tub of Winken, Blinken, and
Nod, the sea roiling as I
recall those wild, wild
nights.

Swaddled in the luxury of
memory, my heart in a
port of safety, my soul
yet longs for a repeat of
those tumbling, turbulent nights.

How to Dance with a Bad Dancer

Lead with panache and wear
steel toed dancing shoes. They
make those especially for dance
teachers. Trade secret. Then
tell the bad dancer what a
good job she is doing and
watch her face light up. She
will do better. Tell her what she
is doing right. She becomes
more confident. She steps on
your foot. You say oops, my
fault. She smiles. There is a
shift, she begins to follow in
earnest. That lasts for eight or
twelve beats. You encourage
her again, send warm energy
through your hand to her
back or shoulder. She leans
into the heat. You are dancing.

Mooning the Sun

We fell in love so hard we had
bruises: elbows, knees, even on
our backsides. You know what
I'm talking about. Rug burns. Sore
tongues. Aching backs, lack of
sleep, no desire to eat, so what
do we do at lunchtime? She
swings by in the company van
and we head for Washington
Park. We have our favorite
spot on the circle by the statue
of Sacajawea. Never mind we
were up all night, who cares
we'll be together again in
five hours? I want her now.
A blanket on the floor of
the van, clothes flung here
and there, mooning the
noonday sun. No sooner
do we sit up and reach for
our pants than the city bus
drives by. Full of smiling
passengers, every one of
them eye to eye with an
eyeful.

Suspense

> *Elysium is as far as to*
> *The very nearest room,*
> *If in that room a friend awaits*
> *Felicity or doom.*
> *What fortitude the soul contains,*
> *That it can so endure*
> *The accent of a coming foot,*
> *The opening of a door!*
> ~Emily Dickinson

When you slept upstairs, and
I slept down, I often fantasized
your footsteps on the stairs,
your hand gripping the rail as if
it were my hair. I imagined you
sitting on the edge of my bed,
demanding pleasure that only
I could give.

So real these illusions, my
heart would pound, my breath
come short. When you got out of
bed to use the bathroom, I listened
to the footfalls, not daring to
breathe as I waited for your
hand on my door.

How to Influence Dreams

Say you love me, court me
sweep me off my feet
dance with me, make me laugh
dress up, be cool, do something
I can't do for myself.

Make me moan with longing
sing to me, whistle for me
bake me a cake.

Buy me presents and tell me
I look pretty. Be unable to
gaze at any other woman
when you're with me.

Smell good, have sweet lips
and a hot crotch. Bump and
grind with me, then kiss
me sweetly and say you'll
see me later.

Call me, text me, send me
an email when I least
expect it. Bring me
balloons. Wake me up at
midnight.

Spare

Spare me the details. Give me
love.
Be spare with your descriptions. Give me
essence.
The river flows. The mountain is
high.
I'll cross and climb them both for
you.
Really, do you need to know more than
you are the one?

The Lovers

The rose did caper on her cheek,
Her bodice rose and fell,
Her pretty speech, like drunken men,
Did stagger pitiful.
Her fingers fumbled at her work,
—Her needle would not go;
What ailed so smart a little maid
It puzzled me to know,
Till opposite I spied a cheek
That bore another rose;
Just opposite, another speech
That like the drunkard goes;
A vest that, like the bodice, danced
To the immortal tune,—
Till those two troubled little clocks
Ticked softly into one.
~Emily Dickinson

When two people meet and feel the
spark, anyone with an open
eye can see it, even in the dark.

You warned me that if we clicked
there would be no turning back. I
scoffed, knowing how quickly heat
can fade, but I was wrong.

Desire Returns for a Visit

We burned hot and hotter. We made

waves, then rode them. We surfed
lava, and cooled off in its steam.

Anyone who saw us in the same
room felt the rising temperature,
heard the resounding click.

Tuxedo and Gown (Beautiful)

We were beautiful the day
we went to the prom. The
gay and lesbian prom took
place on June 15, 1984. You
rented a tux, I bought a
vintage gown and let out the
seams. We both had the
loose curls of romance, and
the pink bloom of youth.
Your photographer friend
came to the house and
took professional shots of
you, me, us, my cat, our
flowers, piano, and the
sun streaming in the windows.
You were slim, handsome
in your white shirt, black
tux, cummerbund and tie, I
was voluptuous and beaming
in shell pink tulle, white lace,
rose pink taffeta with satin
undergarments that made
seductive music when I walked.
We look like newlyweds in
that stack of photographs.
There is a shot of our hands
in white-gold filigree rings with

expensive stones, holding hands,
though we were never wed,
only divorced after nineteen
years. On prom day we
were beautiful.

Desire Returns for a Visit

Desire lies dormant like bulbs
under a mantle of winter
waiting only for spring to
awaken her. It isn't spring that
rings. It is the sound of your
voice after a new haircut, a
laugh as you remind me of
bristles awaiting my hand at
your collar. Or a waft of your
fresh soap smell as you exit
the shower, your towel barely
stretched across the expanse
of your breasts, your curly
vee exposed to my wandering
eyes, as I drop my own clothes
in a heap at your damp feet
and dash into the water to
ready myself for your
attentions. Desire is wide
awake in my hands, my
mouth, my own breasts
and limbs as they tingle
with sure knowledge of
what lies ahead. No dark
mystery awaits us only
joyful delights in coming
home to play.

Possession

> *Did the harebell loose her girdle*
> *To the lover bee,*
> *Would the bee the harebell hallow*
> *Much as formerly?*
> *Did the paradise, persuaded,*
> *Yield her moat of pearl,*
> *Would the Eden be an Eden,*
> *Or the earl an earl?*
> ~Emily Dickinson

Will you still love me tomorrow? When the light dawns, streaking across my face, will you desire me as much as before?

I give you my heart, daring you to break it. Tonight we stretch for paradise. Will you reach for me tomorrow?

Night and Day

> *A shady friend for torrid days*
> *Is easier to find*
> *Than one of higher temperature*
> *For frigid hour of mind.*
> *The vane a little to the east*
> *Scares muslin souls away;*
> *If broadcloth breasts are firmer*
> *Than those of organdy,*
> *Who is to blame?*
> *The weaver?*
> *Ah! the bewildering thread!*
> *The tapestries of paradise*
> *So notelessly are made!*
> ~Emily Dickinson

Hot days require a bit of
linen, a bolt of chambray,
a yard of silk, two of
cotton, always easy to
find. When the east wind
blows in, one seeks a
hardier drape, a woven
wool, straight from the
Kashmir goat, or the Irish
sheep with its lanolin to shed
rain. Nights require a different
warmth, a shadier cool, a
dark corner with a warm
friend. A different animal.

Celebration Time

> *The heart asks pleasure first,*
> *And then, excuse from pain;*
> *And then, those little anodynes*
> *That deaden suffering;*
> *And then, to go to sleep;*
> *And then, if it should be*
> *The will of its Inquisitor,*
> *The liberty to die.*
> ~Emily Dickinson

Dance until our feet refuse to
move, then we bemoan the
pain. Have another glass! Maybe
champagne will deaden those abused
appendages crying for
relief.

We fall into bed, laughing,
loving until early light. Awaken
with the world's greatest
hangover.

Oh goddess, we cry. I've never
been so happy. Please, just
kill me now.

Grappling

Ready to Dwell

If I bide, abide or
exist, hole up, inhabit,
reside or squat here – if I
bunk, continue, crash and
flop, locate, lodge, nest or
occupy. If I park, perch, or
quarter with you, will you
remain, rent, rest, room, and
settle down? Can this be our
sojourn, stay and stop for
once and for all time? If I
hang my hat and give you my
heart, will this be our forever
home?

Before Marriage Equality

As with any right or privilege
those who have always had it
take it for granted, enter into it
lightly or not, depending on their
mood at the time. Maybe they
marry for the lavish wedding because
they've dreamed of wearing that
dress, or instead they run away to
Las Vegas and marry for a mere
fifty-five hours on a drunken whim.
When you don't have that right
you're an outsider not allowed to
call your person your wife, your
husband. Only your partner or
sweetheart or friend. Your honey
or roommate. You may live together
for fifty or a hundred years. But
when one of you is dying in a
hospital bed, watch out for the
short shrift. Your lover's brother
may be told of her death before
you are. Her body may not be
released to your care, no matter
the plans the two of you filed
with your lawyer. When my
daughter told me she was marrying

a man she'd met just three weeks
earlier, after living with women up
until then, I asked her why, why,
why beloved why? The answer
was: because I can.

In the Dark

Everything you ever say
in the dark I say in
the daylight but that
sends you scurrying
like a silverfish
for your moldy book
or a thick new tome
never willing to
face the poetics
of the night in the
light of the day.

Under the moon or
the starless velvet
skies I hear your
silken or hoarse
whispers of desire
flattering phrases
describing my limbs
my skin, my moist
proof of yearning
for your touch.

When I am moved to
sing these same psalms
in the morning rays
to you, to your
neck, your shoulders,

your smell, that
place you called
your bathing suit
area when we were
children together . . .
you need to read
and I am left to
sing my aria to
the window above the
sink as I make our
morning tea.

Compensation

> *For each ecstatic instant*
> *We must an anguish pay*
> *In keen and quivering ratio*
> *To the ecstasy.*
>
> *For each beloved hour*
> *Sharp pittances of years,*
> *Bitter contested farthings*
> *And coffers heaped with tears.*
> ~Emily Dickinson

For every moment spent in
ecstasy, we labored through
months of doubt, counting not our
blessings, but the curses we
heaped upon each other.

For an hour of bliss, we paid
with years of bitter, sharp words,
lonely in each other's company,
waiting for one more ecstatic
instant, one more hour of joy.

Valentine's Day Passion

standing at the pay phone on fifth avenue
eyes filled with tears voice quavering
knees knocking hands shaking I'm torn
apart with passion of the wrong kind

How Do You Want to be Saved?

Shall I save you with my arms and
hold you next to my heart, breathing
onto your soft hair, my tears falling
on your hot head? Or do you prefer
that I save only photos and mementoes
from your life in a scrapbook of purple
velvet, like the one from the theatre
company where we first met? Where
you were confused about your feelings
for me because I looked too butch?

Maybe you don't need saving at
all, but are completely capable of
standing on your own sore feet at
last, it's only that you don't know
it yet you're so used to crying for
help.

The Air Up There

> *Love—thou art high,*
> *I cannot climb thee . . .*
> ~Emily Dickinson

Once I saw you as a meadow,
strewn with boulders, and I a
skipping girl with nothing to keep
me from exploring and conquering
every inch.

You were a grassy plain, covered in
wildflowers whose scent drew me
like a bee, like a butterfly, like the
naïf I was.

I loved the boulders, even though
they hindered my way to
myself.

As time passed, the earth moved,
heaved a bit, and pushed you away
from me. Until . . .

You became a mountain I am not
able to climb. The oxygen is too
thin, my breath too shallow. My

Life too short.

Dream of Heaven

> *Except the heaven had come so near,*
> *So seemed to choose my door,*
> *The distance would not haunt me so;*
> *I had not hoped before.*
> *But just to hear the grace depart*
> *I never thought to see,*
> *Afflicts me with a double loss;*
> *'T is lost, and lost to me.*
> ~Emily Dickinson

In love with love I strove for too many years to reach the heaven I thought was near. My dream was of a happy wife, a life filled with adventure, support, love, affection, and romantic surprise. My days were filled with strife, unhappy conflict, unease, occasional romance, periodic laughter. Ending the difficult marriage was more painful than the living through it. A double loss. Loss of the woman, loss of the dream.

Tweedledum and Tweedledee

Tweedledum and Tweedledee
we bumped butts in our orange-countered
kitchen. Excuse me, excuse me
we laughed as we squeezed around
each other, unnecessarily.
Those were the fun days.

After many years apart
I suddenly remember
the fun days.
After forgiveness
I can recall
the fun days.

Tweedledee and Tweedledum
bumping butts in the kitchen
where we cooked together
lived together and
grew apart together.

Those were the fun days.

Two Women Cooking for Fifty States, or Marriage Equality

Cooking for fifty states and the District of
Columbia the day it becomes legal for these
two women loving women to marry each
other, because that's how we celebrate.
We'll make her delicious macaroni salad
with black olives and my Aunt Inez's
famous old-fashioned southern butter
cake in thirteen-inch pans, then we'll bake
her mom's chocolate chip cookies that are
soft in the middle and crispy on the edges
and my New York cheesecake that takes
me all day long, and her pumpkin soup
that takes a whole jar of peanut butter,
and that recipe from her friend in Maine
that keeps me up all night with indigestion.
In the morning we'll have an overnight
casserole from a recipe her friend's
brother gave us when we visited him
in Illinois. Arizona provides us with
a recipe for trail mix and iced tea,
Alaska another cookie recipe I got
from a hippie friend back in the 70s,
oh I could go on all night, and believe
me we will when that happy day finally
comes. We'll make enough food to
feed all our friends, all our allies,
to remember all the years we've
waited for this minor right.

Texas

Five days after we moved back in together, "You'd better go back to beautiful Texas," I said to my ex as we sat on the back deck crying over the errors of our different ways. It was another year before we were able to call it quits. The path of our togetherness was strewn with rocks rather than the warm sands of true love. Seven years after we broke up she has once again arrived on my doorstep. This time there will be no moving in, only moving on from the dream we each had, which was not the same. I longed for a partner who understood the real me. Who would provide the emotional, loving support I wanted to help me become myself. I don't know what she wanted, really. We talked but never seemed to hear. Now we try to listen to each other. Now, when she knocks, I open the door to my friend. "Welcome back from Texas, beautiful, " I say.

Thirty Years

We are. We are, yes. Yes, we are
just that wild. Just that. Wild.
Maybe it was all those years we
found our relationship on the rocks.
Banging our hearts on the walls. But
now. Now is different. Now, we
laugh at ourselves for the stunts
which used to make us fume.

That time you came back to bed in
the middle of the night, and told me to
wake up and get under the sheet. It
was you underneath the fitted sheet
all along. I was so righteous
then and so tickled now.

You join me in laughing about the
time I was reading in bed, my nightly
wont, and when I couldn't see the
words, dug out my new reading
glasses. Convinced I finally needed
them. (I still don't.) Put them on
top of my distance glasses that
were still on my face.

But. You were nowhere to be seen
that night. It was after we had broken
up and moved apart.

Somehow time worked its magic
and changed our perception.
Now best friends, we go to the shore
and laugh at the couple who were never
able to make it past the rocks.

Surrender

I once lived tethered to the place
where I was born, raised and yearned
for freedom to take flight. I sought
to discover new lands, to take in
every sight, to plant my flag in
prime territory.

I traveled far, both in reality and in
fantasy. I threw myself into each
site, opened bare my heart to every
monarch of the realm. I wandered
and conquered and saw with my
soul the emptiness which lay before
me.

Then I found you. Together we
explored the beauties of remaining
steadfast. We rode the high waves
and crashed on the rocky shores. We
pulled together until we could no
longer hold on. Then we were
dashed apart.

Will I surrender to this land, the
accustomed country of your body?

I miss your hills and curves. I yearn
to return to the familiar. My heart

sends out its sonic beams, calling for
the return of yours. Broad daylight
shows clearly: there is too much
water and no bridge.

Birthday Celebration

Tonight I'll take you to a restaurant, one of your favorites, I'll sing you a medley of all our favorite songs, we'll dance down the urban streets, laughing in the glow of Christmas lights. We'll decry the semi truck with the lights that make its eighteen wheels appear to spin, and recall the nights we walked these streets so many years ago. We'll think of the dogs that walked alongside, now existing only in memory. We'll push away the memories of our quarrels that nearly broke us, the house where only one of us was ever happy. Both of us possess great prowess in this war of push/pull. Let's put on our medals and enjoy the anniversary of your birth.

Witnessing Marriage Equality

There was a time when I
believed marriage between
two people who loved each
other and were deeply committed
for life would never happen. Not
in my lifetime. Not in my country.
Women I knew had been together
for decades, loving, supporting,
fighting and forgiving each other
the same as any couple composed of
one man, one woman.
There was a time when marriage of
same sex couples happened only
before their friends, rarely family, and
never before a judge.
But last May tenth, I stood with my
friend as her witness, as she traded
vows with her partner of thirty years.
Right here in our own country.
My handkerchief was tucked away in
my purse on that bench over there.
So my tears flowed freely down my
cheeks, nowhere to hide, no need to
hide. They bore witness to this
changing time.

Desire Returns for a Visit

Breaking

Language of Flowers

The moment we first kissed, I sent you a
field of coreopsis, arkansas, even though
we lived in Oregon, for this was love at
first sight—where sight means touch.
Myrtle was next, and melianthus.
I signaled you with this forget-me-not,
whose meaning is true love, to let you
know my devotion is complete and I'd never
stray. With honeysuckle, I bound you
to my heart.

Over the years, I sent you a garden, full
of red roses, tulips, and double pinks. They
did their best to climb the rocks, to cover
the weeds and rough patches. When we
tilled it under and planted yellow tulips,
I burned down the house.

Now you've returned from your seven-
year, thousand-mile sojourn. We have
recovered from our wounds, repaired
our hearts, and once again, I signal
you with forget-me-not.

Sweetbitter Unmanageable Creature

Sweetbitter unmanageable creature who
steals in the night, invades my dreams
rips my heart through from its cage
shreds it to strings, then
plucks them like the harp you
strummed daily since childhood.

Your song so familiar throughout
these valleys, a chorus arises to
dance among stargazer lilies of the
field. I can neither gaze nor dance.

Your melody once sweet has soured
Release me from your
adamantine hold. This isn't love.

A Gift-Giving Occasion

Ten years together
eight of them rocky
as the seventh level of
hell and now you say
let's wait to celebrate
and I say no ten
years is now not
later and I want a
diamond tennis bracelet.
You surprise me with it.
I am indeed surprised
because what I
really wanted was
to see the
back of you.

Shimmering

You were still here. In
body. You lay in your room
sleeping, reading, sulking.

I opened my dresser, that one
drawer. I spread everything
on the bed. Red satin tap
pants, red lace bra that opened
in the front, with a heart.
Black silk camisoles, black
satin nightgowns, pink silk
underwear, and those four-inch
heels with ankle straps that I
only ever wore in bed.

Memories lay shimmering,
daring me to don the gear
one more time.

Instead, I gathered the lot
into my arms and filled a
black plastic bag. I added
one last love note:
Honey, remember to take
out the garbage.

That Faraway Look

Only someone whose heart has already been
broken will recognize the look in her eyes
when she sits before the window, yearning
for something or someone who is not
here. I come in the door from work, hoping
for a warm welcome. Instead she looks
through me, past me, around me, searching
for who or what lies beyond. My heart's
scars stretch and tear because her longing
isn't anything I can fix. Has nothing to do
with me. Nothing but the dead
give-away in my chest.

Quitting Time

> *Alter? When the hills do.*
> *Falter? When the sun*
> *Question if his glory*
> *Be the perfect one.*
>
> *Surfeit? When the daffodil*
> *Doth of the dew:*
> *Even as herself, O friend!*
> *I will of you!*
> ~Emily Dickinson

When will I leave you? Let
me count the days:
When the hills give up
their shadows.
When the ocean ceases
its waves.

How will I know I have had
enough? Let me recount
the ways: When the stars
lose their shine.

When the morning dew
refuses to kiss the ground
you walk on.

Then. Then it will be
time.

Too Soon Old

Victory comes late,
And is held low to freezing lips
Too rapt with frost
To take it. How sweet it would have tasted,
Just a drop! Was God so economical?
His table's spread too high for us
Unless we dine on tip-toe.
Crumbs fit such little mouths,
Cherries suit robins;
The eagle's golden breakfast
Strangles them. God keeps his oath to sparrows,
Who of little love
Know how to starve!
~Emily Dickinson

Where have you been all my life
she asked. At last I've found you,
she said. And we clung to each other
on a raft in a vast, churning
ocean. We focused on survival, neglecting
to notice we were drifting apart.

Now it is too late. We are held in aging bodies,
each fighting against time. How can we dance,
make love, make up for
lost years, when we struggle to
roll over in bed.

I look to the sparrows. Learn how
to starve.

The Power of Love

If you were coming in the fall,
I'd brush the summer by
With half a smile and half a spurn,
As housewives do a fly.
If I could see you in a year,
I'd wind the months in balls,
And put them each in separate drawers,
Until their time befalls.
If only centuries delayed,
I'd count them on my hand,
Subtracting till my fingers dropped
Into Van Diemen's land.
If certain, when this life was out,
That yours and mine should be,
I'd toss it yonder like a rind,
And taste eternity.
~Emily Dickinson

We were partners for almost nineteen years. We lived apart for almost half that time, years at a time. Sometimes at a great distance, sometimes in the same city. Had we been allowed to marry, we would no doubt have been divorced.

And yet we remain bound together as surely as if the strands of our

lives had been knitted with small
needles, and never come loose, no
matter how we pick at the pattern.

Society has stopped
blinding its eye, stopped denying the
power of love.

Today we could marry, divorce, live
together or not. We remain separate,
but bound.

Dependency

> *I have no life but this,*
> *To lead it here;*
> *Nor any death, but lest*
> *Dispelled from there;*
> *Nor tie to earths to come,*
> *Nor action new,*
> *Except through this extent,*
> *The realm of you.*
> ~Emily Dickinson

The psychologists called it
co-dependency. I called it life.
Life with you. If you were happy
I was happy. When you felt a
loss, I tried to fill it with purchases
made at any expense, racking up
debt to fill a void I hadn't made.

The psychologists say that when a
person has missed a mother's love
they will always feel the loss. Most
will substitute drugs, alcohol, sex,
or constant buying.

I lived in your realm of bereavement
for more years than either of us
could afford. Gifts never enough,
and all tossed aside when I left.

I lived. I learned. It's only money.
And therein lies the truth: it's only
money—it can never replace the
mother's love of which you were
bereft.

Loving a Survivor

When you were ready to face the past
you turned away from me. I was
devastated by the loss, but fighting
a war is a plausible excuse for absence.
You came back after several years:
scarred, missing parts of yourself
I never knew. I should have given
you a medal. Instead, I offered my
own scarred heart.

Holding

Here I am holding your
goodbye note. If I look
amused, it's because you
tickle me with your conviction
that you have left me and our
relationship behind.
You'll be back.

I drop your note into
the well.

Here I am holding your
heart in my hand. If I seem
undecided, it's because I
want to toss it up, catch it
or not. Maybe I'll jump on
it and break it.
You broke mine.

Here I am holding the
pieces of each of our
hearts. If I look
bewildered, it's because I
don't know how to put
them back together.
You take everything.

Here I am holding a

Desire Returns for a Visit

pen in my hand. Hovering
over my goodbye note.

If I appear heartbroken,
it's because you're holding
the pieces of my life in a
bowl, lifting each one and
feeding it to the
monster at the bottom of
the well.

Don't Forget

You're cleaning out the closets with
vehemence leaving six inches between
shirts. You've tossed out all your brand
name shoes but three pair: dress flats,
sneakers, and boat shoes. You cleaned
cupboards until nothing is left with a
sell-by date that is in the past or less
than a month away. There are only
three magazines left on the coffee
table, and you sent our ancient dog
to live with your mother. I have
one thing to say as I walk out the
door: remember to let go
of yesterday.

Crying in the Face of Rain

The last time we made love I
thought we were just dawning
I told you that night I felt
treasured, taken care of in a
way that I had never before
experienced. Maybe that's why
you couldn't pretend any longer.
You disappeared like the sun
behind the many clouds of
Portland, and I was left
crying in the face of rain.

and then I said . . .

you don't ever want to
see me again. It's not me
it's you. You tried to make
it work, you really did
but you just aren't feeling
it. You thought you loved
me, and when you had
doubts you thought you
would grow to love me.
The sex was great, I
don't need to have any
worries there, it's all you,
you just can't trust anyone.
It's a shame really, you
want to commit, you
want a wife, you want to
make a home. But you
just can't handle any
unpleasantness, any
arguments or anything
like that. I understand,
right? what could I say?
I'll be fine, find someone
else, I'm not too old, I
still have it, have time, and
rest assured, it was
not my fault.

Donations

They do me no good now these
black lace undergarments still
wafting their scent of expensive
hotels and up all night dancing
in rooms with lamps draped with
red lace scarves. No help comes
pouring forth from the four-inch
heels with narrow ankle straps or
the sheer silk peignoir bearing
your handprint on the shoulder
where you steered me onto the
bed that one last time. What use
is it to me to recall the city lights
from iron-railed balconies in the
rain, or black rivers filled with
sailboats full of lovers? My pail of
dreams has been tipped out,
rusted shut and sealed in a
vault of no-more-lies. These
things can go to Goodwill.

Looking Through Stained Glass

Every time I look at the three graces
the handmade art piece, the three
women I wanted and you bought me
for our first anniversary, I remember
our life together as if I were dying: our
life flashes before my eyes, not in
transparency, but through glass stained
with the lies I told myself down the
years. I wanted them to be true, never
doubt that. I built them from dreams
because I didn't have whole cloth. You
were the closest to being my other half,
but I was never the half I thought I was.
I see that now.

Lost in Translation

Beside the Black Sea, I said
you made me feel loved. I cried
in your arms as I confessed the
strength of my feelings for you.
Now I know the night was your
secret goodbye. You came for the
sea, not me.

Storms

Lightning flashed and thunder roared all
night, shaking the brick house where I
lay awake trembling in fear, yearning
for you to come to comfort me. The
you I longed for never existed except
in fairy tales. It was not your job to
comfort me, and your heart was as
full of cracks as my own. Sooner or
later they were bound to break in
storms of our own making.

You Hurt Me

Everything about you agonizes my head. I have a migraine thinking about you.

Everything about you aggrieves my teeth. I grind my molars into crumbs trying to get out of this relationship.

Everything about you distresses my neck. I've been so tense since I met you my vertebrae have fused.

Everything about you pains my shoulders. The deltoid tendons and fibers, the pectoralis no longer know how to shape to fit my shirt.

Everything about you breaks my heart. I spend days and nights and years wanting you, waiting for us to be this pair of swans who mated for life. We are not they.

I won't go on naming body parts that ache because of you. You haven't done this on your own. I am a partner in this crime. This long con. And now

Everything about you tests my sanity. It is time to stop fooling ourselves and move on.

Divorce

Last night just as I was about to
drift off to sleep I awoke with a
thought that sickened me. You
threatened me with your love.
You are coming back into my
life and on your own terms. I
offered you my body and now
you are taking my soul. I knew
I did know and I went ahead
anyway. Thinking I could
handle you. Thinking you had
changed. Now I'm faced with
ugly truth and no choice. No
choice but to hurt you or to be
shackled in a relationship of
pain I neither want nor deserve.
I divorce thee, I divorce thee,
I divorce thee.

Use as Indicated

You should wear a warning label on your heart. List all the troubling side effects, maladies, potential morbidities loving you can cause. There is a reason women never want to see you again, or die of broken hearts, or become stalkers. You dance into our lonely lives, teeth flashing, eyes sparkling, kisses at the ready. You flatter, tease, show yourself at your dazzling best. Then expiry date comes and all is lost. You turn sullen, prickly, too touchy to be touched. We cannot cajole the answer from you because you haven't found it in your long life. If a woman had a choice, she might read the warning label.

Pity Party

The uproar came like hot butter. Smooth, unmarked from the outside, silent turbulence in my heart. The occasion was my departure. For the first and only time, I was the one to leave. Nothing from her but a brief period of anger. And a declaration: we were long over. I had failed as a partner, now I was failing as a friend. She didn't understand why I was grieving now. Too much. Too late.

I'm never on time for the party.

Keeping Apart

> *I cannot live with you,*
> *It would be life,*
> *And life is over there*
> *Behind the shelf...*
> *So we must keep apart,*
> *You there, I here,*
> *With just the door ajar*
> *That oceans are...*
> ~Emily Dickinson

Like the oceans and seas of the
Earth, we cannot mingle our
waters, unless the
continents shift. I cannot live
with you. That life is more
than I am able.

And yet, I sometimes find myself
adrift in the dream. Of what might
have been. Of what might yet
be.

We keep the door ajar, letting
light tease us both. And pray
no shadows fall.

No Time Like the Present

> *I had no time to hate, because*
> *The grave would hinder me,*
> *And life was not so ample*
> *I Could finish enmity.*
> *Nor had I time to love; but since*
> *Some industry must be,*
> *The little toil of love, I thought,*
> *Was large enough for me.*
> ~Emily Dickinson

My beloved and I are born of the same material as all the rest of this universe: stardust. We all glide, slide, haphazard in the chaos we call life, death, time. All a construct we cling to, pray to, sing to. I'll have none of it. I'll have more, please.

Living

Desire Returns for a Visit

The Biology of Co-Dependent Love

                    I served my time. Not in
prison, but in a lockup for women who love too
much. A metaphorical place that feels like
my torso. Sometimes my heart looks like a
bird in a cage. Pecking at her food, spending
time looking in the mirror, asking what did
I do wrong? She swings, not in joy, but in
sorrow, using her clipped wings and still
powerful legs to travel the few inches back
and forth. Other times, my heart sinks to
my pelvic floor, slithers around like a
coral snake, hoping to strike and kill a
blind black snake, and eat until she can
no longer move. When the hunger is too
strong, I sacrifice my own fingers.
I spent nineteen years in the prison of
love. When I emerged, blinking into the
light, I looked into a mirror, and saw an
old woman. Still hungry, but lacking
allure. I can tell my heart it's never too
late, but she knows a lie when she hears
one. She swings, she pecks, she slithers.
She lives, unpardoned.

Love Lifted Me

All I ever learned from love was
how to listen with my fingers, with
my eyes, my hair, my stomach.

All I ever learned from love was how
to ache, to cry, to reach out to the
universe for more lessons.

All I ever learned from love was how
to love back by giving, sharing,
forgiving, and accepting what love
had to offer. I wanted perfection,
peace, support, protection, and to
be heard.

All I ever learned from love
was to provide what I want.

Apocalypse

> *I'm wife; I've finished that,*
> *That other state; I'm Czar,*
> *I'm woman now: It's safer so.*
> *How odd the girl's life looks*
> *Behind this soft eclipse!*
> *I think that earth seems so*
> *To those in heaven now.*
> *This being comfort, then*
> *That other kind was pain;*
> *But why compare?*
> *I'm wife! stop there!*
> ~Emily Dickinson

In the time before we were
allowed to marry, I was her
wife, and she was mine. We
were no longer girls, we were
women, and we wanted a
home. We wanted a soft
place, acceptance from our
neighbors, fun with our
pets.

Long before acceptance came
knocking down doors, we
ran aground on the rocky

shores, older, wiser, and
emotionally bruised.

Now we have no wife. We have
steered our way back to the beginning
place. Like the girls we once
were, we are best friends.

Invitation

Your scent is elusive, not perfume
but I remember it.
You pierced my heart,
and I was bound to you.
I felt intimidated by your strength.
You have no time for cowards
or those who cannot speak up
for themselves.
This trait of yours both buoyed
my spirit
and left me bereft
when I was the one afraid to speak.
I felt you didn't hear me
even when I came in peace.

You are who you are. I am I.
We were meant to be
lifelong friends
our partnership
up in smoke.
Now I long for trysts
the flights of fancy
we have to fly for.
Abundant
in what is now sparse
maybe piercing
my heart, but abundant.
Your prickly embraces
damaged but soft.

Last Dance of the Blue Moon

Tonight a blue moon will shine in
Portland and I will not be there for
the last blue moon with my last
partner. As I drive away from Oregon
for the last time, I will leave all my
exes behind as they all followed me
there even the ones who lived in
other states. I no longer long for a
lover, a partner, a wife. I long for my
self, my freedom, long walks on the
beach in the sun. Swimming alone at
midnight. Thinking deep thoughts
and writing them down to share
on paper. I dream of dancing with
my arms flung wide, open to all
opportunities.

Do You Know the Way?

The way to a man's heart is through
his stomach, they say. But do you know
the way to a woman's? It could be by
cooking her a great meal. It could be by
rubbing her feet. Maybe great sex would
do the trick, but I don't think so. I
think it's the big things like pulling your
weight without being asked, like it's your
job. I think it's by assuming equal
responsibility for the relationship, then
adding small things like appreciation for
her doing her half.

No one ever wrote songs for you to make
yourself handsome at the end of a hard
day, to keep your troubles to yourself, to
keep the children quiet for her sake when
she walks in the door. No one expects you
to do your marital duty regardless of her
skill in this area. If she comes in drunk and
mean after having beers with her peers after
work, you don't have to have kept her
dinner warm, and put up with her lack
of control.

So, yeah, I know the way. And now you
do too. Wanna go pick up some women?

You Get What You Pay For
(and pay for what you get)

If you look back over my
lifetime of loving, you might
think I'd picked up most of my
lovers at a yard sale. They were
never the right fit, always a bit
worn, and if still unused, it was for
a good reason.

Some of them faced a rapid turn
around. I put them right back out
in the yard in a box marked
FREE. Some of them lent themselves
to my friends, as if I were that kind
of woman.

One or two abused me and my
children, strangling us with their
extra-long sleeves, tight knits, and
zippers that wouldn't stay up.

I was well and truly grown up the
day I realized I could choose my own
lovers of the correct fit by shopping
somewhere other than resale.

You're Gone

Now that you're gone, I can
sleep in the middle of the bed.
But I don't. I could cook for one.
But I can't. I'm able to stay up as late
as I choose, read with all the lights
on, make noise in the middle of
the night, tappy tap tap on the
computer as early as I please. I
can stay up all night, go out with
the girls—or the boys for that
matter. I can run up my charge
card, forget to fill up the gas
tank, track in a wheelbarrow of
mud, and believe me, no one
cares. No one yells at me, no
one leaves her socks under the
bed, no one promises to do
the laundry later, or to read my
work and never do it.
No one tells me when my label
is sticking out, or my hair is
funny in the back, or I've said
the wrong word. No one is there
when my mammogram results
come in. Now that you're gone
I take care of myself.

Hope

When I opened my hope chest too
soon I found no trousseau, no good
china, no silver, no linens embroidered
with silk thread, no handmade or
heirloom lace. Fifteen and already
expecting my first child, I found the
chest as lacking in a map of my
future as I was in experience.

Unaware of my role as
architect of my fate, drifting without
a compass, I stumbled on a path of
shards, flames licking at me as if I
were pursued by dragons. My princes
were all frogs, every fork in the road
another way to Nowheresville.

Still that thing within me leaped at every
glimmer of light, it had no feathers, yet
it beat within my chest until I
learned to fly.

Immortal Love

> *That I did always love,*
> *I bring thee proof:*
> *That till I loved*
> *I did not love enough.*
>
> *That I shall love always,*
> *I offer thee*
> *That love is life,*
> *And life hath immortality . . .*
> ~Emily Dickinson

We covered each other in an
avalanche of cards, gifts,
flowers, every romantic
gesture imagined.

We were faithful, loyal, devoted
to each other, no matter the
rocks in our path.

We made each other laugh, no
matter the darkness surrounding
us.

After we broke up, I came
back as your friend. And you
came back as mine.

We have proved our love's
immortality.

Both Sides Now

> *When I hoped I feared,*
> *Since I hoped I dared;*
> *Everywhere alone*
> *As a church remain;*
> *Spectre cannot harm,*
> *Serpent cannot charm;*
> *He deposes doom,*
> *Who hath suffered him.*
> ~Emily Dickinson

When I was younger, I
hoped, and was yet afraid.
But hope gave me courage
to dare, to dare to strike out
alone.
And now alone, as solitary as
a church in a wild wood, I
have no fear of those ghosts
of my childhood. No worry
I will fall victim to the charms
of the snakes of my young
adulthood.
We who once suffered those
cads, now toss them aside.

The Lost Jewel

> *I held a jewel in my fingers*
> *And went to sleep.*
> *The day was warm, and winds were prosy;*
> *I said: "T will keep."*
> *I woke and chid my honest fingers,*
> *—The gem was gone;*
> *And now an amethyst remembrance*
> *Is all I own.*
> ~Emily Dickinson

Remembering those times in a
lavender haze, feelings as gauzy as
curtains surrounding the years, I
feel warm, but sad. Happy for what
we had, despondent for what we
chased, never caught.

I am awake now to what we had,
as well as to what we lacked. Do I
chide myself for wasted time, for
chasing a dream?

Or shall I enjoy the remembrance?

The Contract

> *I gave myself to him,*
> *And took himself for pay.*
> *The solemn contract of a life*
> *Was ratified this way . . .*
> ~Emily Dickinson

In love with love itself,
afraid to live alone, seeking
always for a savior, I began
my life as a victim. This
could have gone wrong, and
it did.

Then one day, with help from
friends and therapy, I broke
the contract with love, and
signed one with myself.

and thus learned to say no to
sacrifice, to say yes to commitment,
to feel real love.

Now my contract is with
the one, and we are all
one.

One is Enough

Few get enough,
—enough is one;
To that ethereal throng
Have not each one of us the right
To stealthily belong?
~Emily Dickinson

If one is enough, why did it take me so many
years to find the one?
I loved a throng of men and
women before I stumbled into your
arms, no longer optimistic, still seeking
the one.

I was a serial romantic, opening my
heart to anyone who showed an
attraction. I wanted—in the worst
way—to belong to that select group
who loved only one. Forever.

Until I learned to love myself, I never knew
true love. At long last I came to understand:
I am the one. I am enough.

Desire Returns for a Visit

Epilogue

Dead Reckoning

Sailors look back to where they started
and every point between, in order to
deduce their current location.

Where am I now on this documented
path of love? The first time, oh the
first time — I fell into a bottomless

pool of stars and swam my way
home, frolicking with dolphins
with cephalopods, with those

mischievous octopussies.
The second time, I was at
one with the sea. I swam with

sharks, restless, not stopping
until I found a companion
who brought art and music

and laughter.
When Pam swam alongside,
with her butchy, bossy manner

we danced, and I was hooked,
tethered to her side
for long years. After we

parted, I dived deep
into my own uncharted
waters. I learned to sleep

while swimming. To breathe
consciously, like a whale.
There are more fish in the

sea, but none are there for me.
Here is where
I am.

About the Author

Sandra de Helen published her first poem at the age of fourteen. Her English teacher, Janice Wallace, submitted the poem to a teacher's magazine and surprised Sandra with a copy in print. The poem was about abortion, which was illegal at the time.

In her twenties, Sandra published a few poems in newspapers, which spurred her to take a Creative Writing Class at the local community college. The [male] professor professed she would never make a good poet because she didn't "write like a man." The next year she joined the women's movement and turned to writing plays.

Forty years later, she picked up Sage Cohen's book, *Writing the Life Poetic: An Invitation to Read and Write Poetry*, and resumed writing poems like a woman.

A long-time resident of Portland, Oregon, Sandra recently relocated to sunny California where she lives with her daughter and a very special cat.

Praise for Other Works by Sandra de Helen

Poetry

"[The poems in *All This Remains to be Discovered*] are a vulnerable, raw look at one's life with an undertone of tenderness and adult compassion and forgiveness. A very moving and worthwhile read."
~BuzzOregon

"I loved how honest and plain all the tales were [in *All This Remains to be Discovered*]. After reading this short book, I felt like I knew, intimately, every important person in the poet's life."
~Amazon.com

Plays

"[The stageplay] *The Clue in the Old Birdbath* is proving to be catnip for the robust, unadorned, unescorted females in attendance. Unfolding is a musical demolition by Sandra de Helen and Kate Kasten of Carolyn Keene's nubile teen detective Nancy Drew, here renamed Tansy True. Here, adolescent literature's beacon of girlish pluck and ingenuity is rendered into a salty, torpedo-breasted assassin of male domination."
~Keith A. Joseph, Cleveland Scene

Novels

"I wish I had half the plotting talent that Sandra de Helen has. [*Till Darkness Comes*] is such a terrific and totally satisfying book."
~Chelsea Cain, Thriller Writer, Humorist, and News Columnist

"[*The Hounding* is a] confident, meticulously detailed mystery that would have made Shirley [Comb's] pipe-smoking idol proud."
~Kirkus Reviews

"*The Hounding* is . . . an interesting and well-developed mystery. I recommend it for any Holmes/Watson obsessives."
~Megan Casey, Lesbrary.com

"If you are a lover of Sherlock Holmes, [*The Illustrious Client*] is a fun look at what might happen had the characters been women and in the present day. The books' titles are taken from Sherlock Holmes' own stories and this book is loosely based on the one of the same title. However, this is not just a retelling of the Holmes stories. Ms. de Helen definitely makes it her own. The clues and red herrings as the pair solve the mystery are well placed. The plot was strong and interesting, and like a really good mystery, I couldn't figure out 'whodunnit' and was surprised by the reveal at the end."
~Long and Short Reviews.com

"[*The Illustrious Client*] is certainly worth a read. With the author continuing to hone her talents, I am looking forward to the next one."
~Megan Casey, Lesbrary.com

Copyright Notes

Versions of some poems in this collection first appeared in the following publications:

"Don't Speak," *Binge Press*, 2012; and *All This Remains to be Discovered*, 2015.

"Dry Season," *Concrete & River*, 2018.

"How to Influence Dreams," *Lavender Review*, Issue 3; *Binge Press*, 2012; and *All This Remains to be Discovered*, 2015.

"In The Dark," *Binge Press*, 2012; and *All This Remains to be Discovered*, 2015.

"Looking Through Stained Glass," *Impossible Archetype*, 2018.

"Tuxedo and Gown (Beautiful)," *All This Remains to be Discovered*, 2015.

www.ingramcontent.com/pod-product-compliance
Lightning Source LLC
Chambersburg PA
CBHW030527080526
44586CB00011B/349